J 977.1 SCH
Schonberg, Marcia.
B is for buckeye : an Ohio
alphabet

W9-BYA-803

FOUNTAINDALE PUBLIC LIBRARY DISTRICT
300 West Briarcliff Road
Bolingbrook, IL 60440-2894
(630) 759-2102

B is for Buckeye

An Ohio Alphabet

Written by Marcia Schonberg and Illustrated by Bruce Langton

Text Copyright © 2000 Marcia Schonberg
Illustrations Copyright © 2000 Bruce Langton

Photo reference for the letter D provided by Hemera.
Photo references for the letters C, G, H, M, U, and Z provided through the photography
of Marcia Schonberg.

All rights reserved. No part of this book may be reproduced in any manner
without the express written consent of the publisher, except in the case of brief
excerpts in critical reviews and articles. All inquiries should be addressed to:

Sleeping Bear Press™

315 E. Eisenhower Parkway, Ste. 200
Ann Arbor, MI 48108
www.sleepingbearpress.com

Sleeping Bear Press, a part of Cengage Learning.

15 14 13 12 11 10 9

Library of Congress Cataloging-in-Publication Data
Schonberg, Marcia.
B is for buckeye: an Ohio alphabet / by Marcia Schonberg.
p. cm.
ISBN 13: 978-1-58536-004-8
1. Ohio–Juvenile literature. 2. English language–Alphabet–Juvenile literature.
[1. Ohio. 2. Alphabet.] I. Title.
F491.3 .S36 2000
977.1–dc21   00-010979

Printed by China Translation & Printing Services Limited,
Guangdong Province, China. 9th Printing. 03/2012

For Brandon and Joel
Adam, David, Lisa, and Jeff—
With special gratitude to Bill, who so lovingly inspires us all.

—Marcia Schonberg

My thanks go out to my parents
for giving me faith and inspiration to be an artist.

My love goes out to my wife Rebecca
and my children Brett and Rory
for being by my side and understanding my desires and dreams.

My gratitude to Sleeping Bear Press and
Marcia Schonberg in helping to make those dreams come true.

—Bruce G. Langton

A is for Astronauts
speeding through space.
They circle the earth and walk on the moon,
exploring a dark and exciting place.

Ohio has produced more astronauts than any other state. Twenty-three Ohioans have flown into outer space, among them John Glenn, who rocketed into the atmosphere aboard the *Friendship 7* on February 20, 1962, to become the first American to circle the earth—and he did it three times. After retiring from the National Aeronautics and Space Administration (NASA), he entered Ohio politics and in 1974 and 1980 was elected to the U.S. Senate. When John Glenn flew into outer space in 1998 aboard the *Discovery*, he became the oldest person to make a space flight.

With people all around the world breathlessly watching TV sets on July 20, 1969, Neil Armstrong became the first person to walk on the moon.

Kathryn Sullivan, who flew aboard the *Challenger* in October 1984, was the first woman to walk in outer space.

In July 1995, a five-person team flew in the shuttle *Discovery* to launch satellites into outer space. Only one of those five adventurers was not an Ohioan, so Governor George Voinovich made Kevin Kregel an honorary citizen of our state to make this an all-Ohio team.

Aa

Ohio is known as the Buckeye State because Buckeye trees grow so abundantly here. William Henry Harrison, the ninth U.S. President, helped introduce the Buckeye to the country in the nineteenth century. Although he was born in Virginia to a wealthy family, during his election year in 1839, Harrison was pictured as a down-to-earth western farmer. Stories claimed that he was born in a log cabin built of the Buckeye tree. In the nation's eyes the connection between Ohio and Buckeye was launched.

Dawes Arboretum in Newark has the "Famous 17"—Buckeye trees planted in the shape of the number 17—as a reminder that in 1803 Ohio became the 17th state to enter the Union.

Native Americans called the shiny brown Buckeye seed "hetuck," meaning "the eye of the buck," because it reminded them of a male deer's eye. The tree can grow to 100 feet in height. Its leaves are large and shaped like palms, with long, showy flower spikes, and large, prickly nuts containing inedible kernels, or buckeyes.

B is for Buckeye,
   Ohio's nickname and tree.
Its nut looks like a deer's eye,
   early pioneers would all agree

From the day it was founded, Columbus has had as many adventures as its daring namesake, Christopher Columbus. The first settlers arrived here in 1797. When Ohio became the 17th state, Chillicothe was named the first state capital, but when farmers in the heart of Ohio offered 1,200 acres of land and $50,000 to build a capitol building and penitentiary, the general assembly voted to move the state government to the banks of the Scioto River. In 1816, 13 years after Ohio became a state, Columbus became its capital.

The Statehouse is where our laws are made; inside the top of the Statehouse rotunda is the Ohio State Seal, created in stained glass.

The red carnation became Ohio's state flower in honor of Ohioan president, William McKinley. One day a friend offered him a bright red carnation to wear in his lapel for good luck, and it must have worked, because from that day on, he always wore the flower. In fact, thanks to his friend's beautiful carnation beds in Alliance, that town became know as Carnation City.

Ohio's state bird is the cardinal, a North American songbird that lives in Ohio all year. Male cardinals can grow to be 9 inches long and are dressed in bright red suits with a crest on their heads and a thick orange-red bill. The females are reddish-brown.

In Ohio many symbols and places start with the letter C, and none could be more important than Columbus, our capital city.

In May, the rare and beautiful Lakeside Daisy blooms along Lake Erie's shore on the Marblehead Peninsula, which is the only place in the United States where the plant grows naturally. The yellow Lakeside Daisy has become the rarest of all endangered plants in Ohio.

Daisy is also one of the oldest and most common name for a dairy cow—perhaps because cows often graze in fields of daisies. Dairy products like milk, cream, and cheese are among Ohio's leading agricultural products, thanks to the thriving dairy farms here. In 1880, the huge production of milk and the 40 cheese factories near Wellington prompted the town to be christened the "Cheese Capital of the United States."

D can be for Dairy cow
in fields grazing
and for Ohio's wildflower
the yellow Lakeside Daisy.

In 1669, French explorer Louis Joliet discovered Lake Erie and for the next 100 years France and England argued about who owned it. The fourth largest of the Great Lakes, Lake Erie is also the shallowest. Its 9,940 square miles separate Ontario, Canada from the United States. Lake Erie is 241 miles long, between 30 and 57 miles wide, and as deep as 210 feet. More than 300 bird species nest in the woods and marshes along the shore and many varieties of wildflowers, mammals, reptiles, and amphibians also make their homes here. Lake Erie has more numbers and varieties of fish than any of the other Great Lakes.

U.S. Naval Officer Oliver Hazard Perry built and manned a fleet of ships on Lake Erie during the War of 1812 that was fought between the United States and Great Britain. The Battle of Lake Erie has been called the most decisive naval battle in history and the biggest battle ever fought on inland waters. In September 1813, near Put-in-Bay, Ohio, Commodore Perry forced the British navy to surrender the entire lake to the United States. His report of the battle became one of history's most famous phrases: "We have met the enemy and they are ours."

The letter E stands for Erie,
a lake that's great fun to explore.
Rocks and sandy beaches have secrets galore
and long ago, battles were once seen offshore.

F is for Flint,
a rock with powers that early man could mint.
Fire and firearms were made with Ohio's gemstone.
So were arrowheads and tools, the earliest ones known.

Flint is Ohio's official gemstone and is the darkest variety of chert, a type of quartz. The stone was first used 15,000 years ago to make knives and spearheads because, although it is very hard, it can easily be shaped by flaking off the edges with a blunt rock or small hammer. Before matches were invented, people would hit steel against flint to strike a spark that would light fires. Gun makers in the seventeenth and eighteenth centuries combined flint and steel to set off the gunpowder in the flintlock guns used by America's early pioneers.

Flint Ridge State Memorial and Museum in Newark preserves pit areas where American Indians once mined flint. The museum traces the mineral from its raw state to its many uses by Native Americans.

Ff

Glacier starts with the letter **G**.
Made of ice and snow,
    it carved hills and valleys
    millions of years ago.

Glaciers created Ohio's many different land formations long before men, women, and children lived on earth. A glacier is a mass of ice formed in high mountains and polar regions. When the snow is compressed it begins to move by the pressure of its own weight. Millions of years ago, the Wisconsin Glacier moved across what would become Ohio, carving gorges, ravines, rock bridges, huge boulders, cliffs, and recessed caves into the landscape. It also formed waterfalls and smoothed the land in northwestern Ohio into flat plains.

Within the 800 acres of Kelleys Island State Park are glacial grooves, where fossilized marine life is embedded in limestone bedrock. These grooves are considered among the finest glacial carvings in America.

H is the letter for this special place
full of butterflies, squirrels, and bees.
Holden Arboretum is nature's delight
with gardens of flowers, plants, and trees.

Arboretum is another word for botanical garden, a public place where plants are grown for people to enjoy and for scientists to study. Arbor is the Latin word for tree, so an arboretum concentrates on woody plants, trees, and shrubs.

The largest arboretum in the United States is located in northeastern Ohio. Holden Arboretum, covering 3,100 acres, has miles of walking trails that weave through its woodland "museum" passing woods, lakes, fields, and ravines. Look for rhododendrons, lilacs, buckeyes, and crab apples along with maples, evergreens, and wildflowers. There is a white oak tree in Holden Arboretum that is more than 350 years old.

Ohio is—and has been—the home of many inventors. Wilbur and Orville Wright invented an airplane that would fly. W.F. Semple patented chewing gum in 1869. Engineer Charles Kettering held 140 patents for his inventions, among them an electric starter that helped in the development of the modern automobile. Granville Woods is sometimes called "Ohio's Forgotten Inventor." He patented more than 50 inventions, including automatic railroad brakes and other electrical devices that made railroads safer.

Many of Ohio's inventors worked on lights. Garrett Morgan invented the first traffic light. Charles Bush created the electric arc light, which replaced earlier gas streetlights. Thomas Edison made an even better electric light. Later, Arthur Compton invented the skinny florescent light tubes we use in schools and homes.

Ii

I is for Inventors,
people who use their imagination.
Their job is to think of something new,
like airplanes, lights, and chewing gum too.

J stands for John Chapman,
    a man who sowed seeds and did good deeds.
Early settlers all agreed
that he deserved the name, Johnny Appleseed.

Johnny Appleseed is one of the best-loved characters in American history and folklore. He was born in Massachusetts in 1774 and was named Johnny Chapman. For 40 years he wandered throughout western Pennsylvania, Ohio, and Indiana, sowing apple seeds that in time grew into orchards enjoyed by pioneers. Legends say that Johnny Appleseed wore his cooking pot on his head as he traveled. In 1840, even though John Chapman settled in a cabin near Mansfield, he continued to wander for hundreds of miles planting apple seeds. Stories about his love of animals and great kindness spread far and wide and he became a legend in his own day. He died in 1845, but a few of the trees he planted still grow in Ohio. He was living proof of his motto: "The good that men do lives after them."

Jj

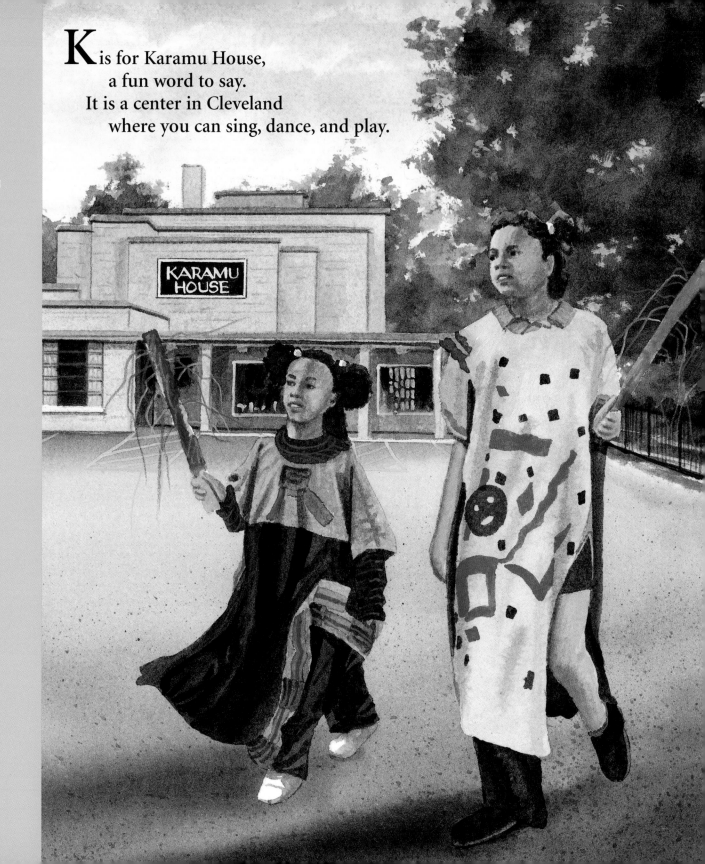

K is for Karamu House,
a fun word to say.
It is a center in Cleveland
where you can sing, dance, and play.

Karamu is a word that means "a place of joyful gatherings" in the Swahili language. The Karamu House in Cleveland is the oldest African-American cultural arts center in the United States. It was founded in 1915 by two graduates of Ohio's Oberlin College, our nation's first coeducational interracial college. Russell and Rowena Woodham Jelliffe wanted to bring people of different backgrounds, races, and religions together to develop their artistic talents. Inside the Karamu House there are theaters, dance and art studios, an art gallery, an early childhood development center, and even a neighborhood bank.

The ladybug, sometimes called a Ladybird Beetle, is Ohio's state insect. Less than a quarter-inch long and round in shape, ladybugs have tiny wings and short legs. Some have red or yellow backs that are covered with black spots. Others have black backs with yellow or red spots. These helpful beetles eat destructive plant-eating insects. They have big appetites and big families, so scientists often call upon them to help stop nature's pests from eating crops and vegetation.

Now we have a special insect
hiding in our book.
What can it be?
Come and take a look!

L stands for Ladybug.
Tiny, red and black,
she wears a cloak of polka dots
upon her round, hard back.

Named for Queen Marie Antoinette of France, Marietta sits where the Muskingum and Ohio rivers meet. Marietta became the first capital of the Northwest Territory. During its early years, many paddleboats moved along the two rivers, ferrying goods and settlers. Several boats in town can be toured.

m
M

M is for Marietta,
    a charming river town
        where crowds gather, bands play,
            and paddle wheels go round and round.

N stands for Nature,
living things in the great outdoors
such as Ohio's prairies and pine forests
as well as scenic lakeshores.

Nature preserves may look like parks, but they are designed and maintained for visitors who fly in with wings or visit on four paws, hooves, or feet. The Ohio Department of Natural Resources protects many of these special areas and asks human visitors to help.

Some nature preserves have unusual rock formations. In Rockbridge State Nature Preserve, a 100-foot rock bridge was formed more than a million years ago. Ohio caverns display pure white stalactites and stalagmites against a backdrop of vividly colored walls. Hocking Hills State Park has recess caves and waterfalls, gorges, rock pools, winding ravines, and other natural formations.

The white-tailed deer, Ohio's state mammal, can be found in all of Ohio's 88 counties. When frightened the white-tailed deer raises its tail, which is white on the underside, as a flag warning family members of possible danger. Fawns recognize their mothers by sniffing the scent glands on their ankles.

Pulitzer Prize winner and Ohio native Louis Bromfield once pointed out, "Ohio is the farthest West of the East and the farthest North of the South."

The name comes from the Iroquois word *Oheyo*, which means "beautiful river" or "great river," and it is indeed a state with many beautiful rivers, as well as rolling pastures, prairies, plateaus, forests, and rocky cliffs.

For centuries, Native American tribes roamed the area. At the end of the French and Indian War in 1763, Great Britain acquired the land and held it until the end of the American Revolution. Once claimed by both Connecticut and Virginia, Ohio became part of the Northwest Territory in 1787. Eventually the area was separated, and in 1803, Ohio was admitted to the Union as the 17th state.

The earliest settlers left their homes in New England, Pennsylvania, Kentucky, and Virginia to move to Ohio. In the 1830s, the German and Swiss arrived. In the 1840s, the Irish followed. The flourishing Amish and Mennonite communities have also helped make Ohio a unique place to live.

O! This one is tricky! See if you can guess:
What's round on the ends and "hi" in the middle?

The answer is OHIO!
Did you figure out the riddle?

Warren G. Harding

William H. Harrison

Ulysses S. Grant

William H. Taft

Rutherford B. Hayes

William McKinley

Benjamin Harrison

James A. Garfield

From Ohio came eight Presidents,
bringing us to the letter **P**.
Two Harrisons, one Hayes,
a Grant and a Garfield,
portly Taft, Harding, and a
carnation-clad McKinley.

Ohio is known as "The Mother of Presidents" because it has sent more men to the White House than any other state. The first president from Ohio was our 9th president, William Henry Harrison (1773-1841). A general during the War of 1812, he won the presidency in 1840.

The 18th president, Ulysses S. Grant (1822-1885) commanded the Union armies during the Civil War.

Rutherford B. Hayes (1822-1893) followed Grant in office, becoming the 19th president.

James A. Garfield (1831-1881) was the 20th president. He was assassinated four months after taking office.

The grandson of William Henry Harrison, Benjamin Harrison (1833-1901) became the 23rd president.

Our 25th president, William McKinley (1843-1901), was a former governor of Ohio before being elected president in 1896. He was assassinated, in Buffalo, during his second term.

William Howard Taft (1857-1930), was the only president to become Chief Justice of the Supreme Court. Taft was elected our 27th president in 1908.

Warren G. Harding (1865-1923), our 29th president of the United States, ran for office in 1921 with the promise to return the country to "normalcy" (a word he made up) after World War I.

Q stands for Quaker Oats,
   Ohio's favorite breakfast food.
Steaming hot and swimming in milk,
   it puts us in a happy mood.

The forerunner of the Quaker Oats Company began in Akron in 1854 by Ferdinand Schumacher, a German immigrant who in time became known as the "Cereal King of America." In 1872, he established the Empire Barley Mill in Akron. Eleven years later, he built an eight-story jumbo mill that covered an entire city block. A devastating fire in 1886 led to a merger with the Akron Milling Company. Then, in 1901, it became a major component of the Quaker Oats Company.

Quaker Oats stopped production in Akron in 1970 and the headquarters moved. Today the 36 huge grain silos are part of the Quaker Square Hilton Hotel, where the silos no longer store oats, wheat, and barley, but rather house 186 rooms for hotel guests. Nearby, a 1938 Broadway Limited train, once used to transport grain to the milling company, displays a collection of railroad memorabilia.

The largest collection of roller coasters in the world can be found at Cedar Point in Sandusky. The 364-acre amusement park opened in 1870 and today has 14 roller coasters. During the first year of the new millennium, Millennium Force opened, a 310-foot high world-record-breaking roller coaster offering a 92-mile-an-hour fright. Cedar Point also has the tallest free-fall ride in the world (the Power Tower with a 300-foot drop) and has 68 amusement rides, the most in one park. There are more than 2,000 trash cans to keep the park clean!

R rolls over the tongue
like a Roller coaster over its rails.
With breathtaking dives
and high-speed glides,
roller coasters give
the most rollicking rides.

Rr

Sstands for Columbus's ship, the *Santa Maria*.
In Fourteen Hundred and Ninety-Two,
she left Spain and sailed the ocean blue
with a fearless captain and a valiant crew.

Ss

Because Columbus was named for explorer Christopher Columbus, in honor of the 500th anniversary of Columbus's trip to America, the mayor of the city commissioned the building of a replica of the explorer's flagship, the *Santa Maria*. It is a wooden ship with three masts and five large sails. Like the original *Santa Maria*, the replica is 98 feet long. Opened for tours in 1992, the *Santa Maria* replica is permanently moored downtown on the Scioto River at Battelle Park.

T is for Tomato
which makes the beverage of Ohio.
Here, tons of tasty tomatoes grow
to produce the juice Ohioans know.

Tomato juice was adopted as the state beverage in 1965. Ohio leads the country in the production of tomato juice and is second only to California in the number of tomatoes grown each summer.

The tomato is actually classified as the fruit of an herb plant in the night-shade family. Before the nineteenth century, settlers believed that the tomato was poisonous and often called it the "love apple." There are many varieties of tomatoes, whose plants produce round or oval fruit that turns either yellow or red when ripe.

The Underground Railroad was not a real train that ran on railroad tracks, but a transportation system made of people helping people. Established before the Civil War when slavery existed in the southern states, the Underground Railroad transported slaves to freedom. Many secret paths wound through the countryside, starting at the Ohio River and curving north to Lake Erie. A candle in a window or a gourd beside a door would indicate that help and food awaited the runaways. These safe houses were called "stations" and the brave Ohioans who helped slaves were known as "conductors." Slaves were not free until they reached Canada on the other side of Lake Erie.

Ohio has many historic sites where slaves stayed; among them are the 1840s Hubbard House in Ashtabula and the Rankin House in Ripley.

Many famous Ohioans fought to free the slaves. Harriet Beecher Stowe of Cincinnati battled slavery with her pen when she wrote *Uncle Tom's Cabin*. The Union's most effective Civil War generals—Ulysses S. Grant, William Tecumseh Sherman, Philip Sheridan, and George Armstrong Custer—were all Ohioans.

Underground Railroad starts with U.
It had no train, no engine,
no whistle that blew.
Hidden "stations" marked by secret clues
and kind "conductors" led slaves
to safe houses they knew.

James Murray Spangler of Canton was a janitor with a brilliant idea. In his day, carpet sweepers were manual, not electric, but he knew electricity would create possibilities for labor-saving devices. In 1907, Spangler built an electric suction sweeper using metal, wood, and a pillowcase as a bag to capture the dirt. After having his invention patented, he sold it to a businessman named William Hoover. Hoover worked from Spangler's prototype and manufactured the first successful portable electric suction sweeper in 1908. In time, the Electric Suction Sweeper Company of New Berlin (now North Canton) became the Hoover Company. Hoover still makes vacuum cleaners, as well as rug cleaners and other floor care items.

Vacuum cleaner begins with V
a favorite for those who go on a cleaning spree.
Push it around after you turn it on
and very soon the dirt is gone.

Aviation pioneers Wilbur and Orville Wright were brothers born in Dayton shortly after the Civil War. In the 1890s, they started manufacturing bicycles, studying aeronautical literature, and experimenting with gliders to learn wind control and lateral balancing. They tested their gliders at Kitty Hawk, N.C., where the winds were known to be fairly constant. On December 17, 1903, Orville made the first flight in a power-driven plane, but the world knew nothing of those 12 precious seconds or the brothers' work until five years later, when a newspaper reporter named D. Bruce Salley witnessed their 1,000-foot flight.

Dayton, the birthplace of aviation, was the Wright brothers' home and the site of the Wright Cycle Company Shop. Nearby, at Huffman Prairie, the Wrights built and tested some of their "flying machines." A memorial and replica of their hangar can be found there today.

W
W

W is for Wright brothers
who dreamt of reaching the sky,
they built planes in their bicycle shop
and became the first inventors to fly.

Once the site of the Shawnee Nations' largest settlement, Xenia is the birthplace of Shawnee Chief Tecumseh. He and his brother, The Prophet, united western Indians to protect their tribal lands and culture from encroaching frontiersmen. Tecumseh was defeated at the Battle of Tippecanoe, where another Ohioan, William Henry Harrison, commanded United States troops. Later Harrison became our 9th president. Another Ohio general, William Tecumseh Sherman, was named for the chief known to be brave in battle.

Xenia is known as the City of Hospitality because its name in Greek means hospitality. It is also known as Trail City USA, after being ranked as one of the best cities in the U.S. to hike, bike, and skate. The trails follow the path of old railroad tracks.

The X word is Xenia
though its X sounds like a Z.
This is Ohio's City of Hospitality
it's also a great place to bike—try it and see.

Y y

The Y bridge spans two rivers
keeping travelers dry.
You can cross the bridge and not the river
though you may be wondering why.

Zanesville sits at the junction of two scenic highways and two rivers, the Muskingum and the Licking. Since 1814, five different bridges have been constructed at the same location over these rivers. The fifth bridge boasts one of the world's most unusual designs. On this three-way overpass, you can indeed cross the bridge without crossing a river. West Main Street, Linden Avenue, and U.S. 40 meet in the middle of the bridge. The best view of this unusual structure is from Putnam Hill Park Overlook.

Ohio has five zoos: Toledo Zoo, Akron Zoological Park, Cleveland Metroparks Zoo, Columbus Zoo, and the Cincinnati Zoo and Botanical Garden. Each provides homes for rare and wonderful creatures from every corner of the world.

The Toledo Zoo was the first zoo in the world to design a "hippoquarium" where visitors can watch the hippos swimming underwater in their see-through tank. It also features a savanna area and a 17,000-square-foot gorilla meadow. At the Columbus and Cincinnati zoos you can see the endangered manatee in specially designed aquariums.

Zz

Z stands for Zoo,
where hippos and manatees are on view.
Visitors can watch alligators chew,
and rare red pandas will wave at you.

Now we've said the ABCs
it is fun as fun can be
and we've discovered Ohio
from the letters A to Z!

A Basket of Buckeye Facts

1. Do you know Ohio's state motto?

2. During the Civil War, only one battle was fought in Ohio. Can you name it? (Hint: It was fought in and along the Ohio River.)

3. In this same battle, three officers who fought together would one day become presidents of the United States. Who are these Ohio presidents?

4. What president from Ohio served the shortest term?

5. Who was our nation's "First Lady?" (Hint: It wasn't Martha Washington.)

6. How many counties are there in Ohio?

7. We learned that Ohio's state flower is the carnation. Do you know the name of our state wildflower? How many petals does it have?

8. What is the highest place in Ohio?

9. Ohio became a state in 1803. How many states did that make?

10. What is the capital of Ohio? Now, where were the earlier capital cities?

11. Ohio has many words taken from the Native Americans who lived here. Can you name the seven settlements who lived here before the Europeans arrived?

12. Which of the Great Lakes is the shallowest?

13. Ohio has a rock song. What is the name of it and what university band made it popular?

14. What is Ohio's state reptile?

15. What does the sun rising above the mountains on "Great Seal of Ohio" stand for? What does the wheat symbolize?

16. What is Ohio's state fossil?

17. Where was the War of 1812 fought in Ohio?

18. An African American from Cleveland, Ohio, Garrett Morgan invented something that made traffic flow more smoothly. Do you know what he invented? (Hint: You probably see at least one every day.)

19. Two bodies of water border Ohio. What are they?

20. What and where is the largest military museum in the world?

Answers:

1. "With God, all things are possible."

2. The Battle of Buffington Island.

3. Rutherford B. Hayes, James Garfield, and William McKinley

4. William Henry Harrison served only 32 days.

5. It was the Lucy Webb Hayes, wife of Rutherford B. Hayes, our 19th president. She was called the "First Lady" by a reporter and the befitting title for presidential wives stuck ever since. She was also the first First Lady to have a college diploma. She graduated from Ohio Wesleyan Women's College in 1850.

6. 88.

7. Our state wildflower, the White Trillium, has three petals.

8. Campbell Hill, near Bellefontaine, Ohio, is the highest point between the Appalachian Mountains and the Mississippi River. It is 1,550 feet above sea level.

9. Ohio became the 17th state.

10. Columbus is the capital. Marietta, Cincinnati, Chillicothe and Zanesville all served as capitals until 1816.

11. Ottawa, Wyandot, Erie, Tuscarora, Miami, Shawnee, and Delaware.

12. Lake Erie.

13. A band in Dayton wrote "Hang on Sloopy," but The Ohio State University Marching Band made it popular in the 1960s and continues to play it each season.

14. The Black Racer Snake, because it can be found in each county.

15. The sun represents Ohio, as the first state west of the Allegheny Mountains. The wheat reminds us of the importance of agriculture in Ohio.

16. It is the trilobite. It is an extinct sea creature that lived in Ohio 440 million years ago when the state was covered with salt water.

17. On Lake Erie. Commodore Oliver Hazard Perry and his American fleet defeated the British near South Bass Island. Today, Perry's Victory and International Peace Memorial salutes the win and also our friendship with Canada which shares Lake Erie as a border.

18. Garrett Morgan invented the traffic light in 1923.

19. Lake Erie on the North and the Ohio River on the South.

20. The United States Air Force Museum in Dayton.